MORE, FEWER, LESS

TANA HOBAN

GREENWILLOW BOOKS  NEW YORK

The full-color photographs were reproduced
from 35-mm slides. Copyright © 1998 by Tana Hoban.
All rights reserved. No part of this book may be
reproduced or utilized in any form or by any means,
electronic or mechanical, including photocopying,
recording, by any information storage and retrieval
system, without permission in writing from the Publisher,
Greenwillow Books, a division of William Morrow
& Company, Inc., 1350 Avenue of the Americas,
New York, NY 10019.
www.williammorrow.com
Printed in Singapore by Tien Wah Press
First Edition 10 9 8 7 6 5 4 3 2 1

Library of Congress Cataloging-in-Publication Data
Hoban, Tana
More, fewer, less / by Tana Hoban.
    p.   cm.
Summary: Photographs illustrate groupings
of objects in larger and smaller numbers.
ISBN 0-688-15693-2 (trade).
ISBN 0-688-15694-0 (lib. bdg.)
1. Set theory—Juvenile literature.   [1. Set theory.]
I. Title.   QA248.H592   1998   511.3'2—dc21
97-36665   CIP   AC

For
Miela

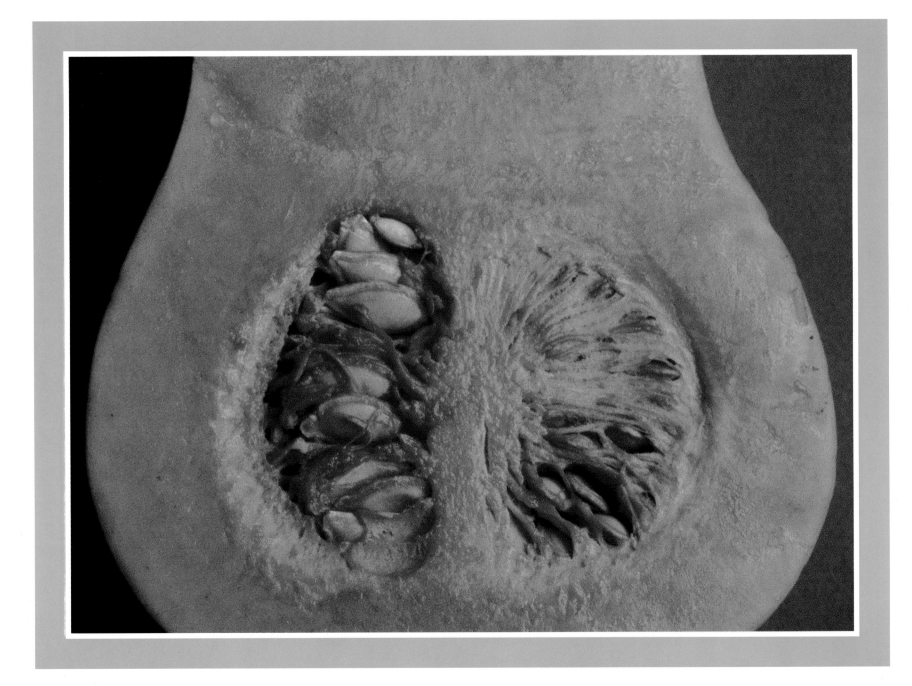